chat

christmas

Kirsten Hart

how to use chat with your small group

I wrote this book hoping that you would read these thoughts and ideas together with a group of friends, and that it would lead to conversations about the Bible and how it applies to our day to day lives. I suppose that's the hope for every Bible study, but I do want this to be slightly different. I hope that you will view your time together as a time of fellowship – intimate fellowship – which is thought provoking and therefore could be incredibly intellectually stimulating.

My favorite times discussing the Bible are with close, fun friends that aren't afraid to 'go there' with certain biblical topics. Explore God's fascinating word! Discussion as a group, versus being led by a single teacher is how I view CHAT being used. Jump around with the topics, if you so choose. These are not chronologically constructed chapters. If you aren't able to attend small group, or Bible study for a week, you really can't get behind.

Open each question in the Chat Time section to the whole group. Take your time with the questions. Wait until everyone has had a chance to 'chime in' before going on to the next question. If you get sidetracked on one question in particular, go with it. Sometimes the best group chats happen when least expected. That's the good stuff.

Take a deep breath. Make some of the yummy dessert recipes from the back of the book, brew some coffee, tea, or cocoa, and enjoy discussing God's word. Chat away!

Contents

chat christmas

chat christmas is a special edition of the chat 'a conversational bible study' series. Usually the chat books contain twelve separate chapters. This Christmas edition only contains four, and is meant as a special study to fit in-between Thanksgiving and Christmas. Designed to concentrate on this time of celebrating Thanksgiving and the birth of our Lord.

Be sure to check out the recipes in the back of each book!

More chat studies are available on my website:
www.KirstenHart.com
Or
www.Amazon.com
(search chat by Kirsten Hart)

traditional style

Not too long ago, I was chatting with both of our adult sons. We were talking about traditions in our immediate family, and apparently (according to my sons), we really don't have any holiday traditions.

"Yes, we do! We all watch ELF at Christmas time, and The Santa Claus movie", I chimed in. But that was a lame attempt to fill in the realization that I had failed my family to a certain degree. I had lacked the forming of longstanding family Christmas traditions. Tyler and Ryan, I am sorry.

During that conversation, I realized that we didn't have an official traditional meal we always eat on Christmas day. (The year of the conversation, Christmas was on a Sunday, so we took the boys out after church to the local Chinese All-You-Can-Eat Buffet for our Christmas Dinner!) Seriously? What's my deal? Worst Christmas meal ever.

Then there's the one year when I bought a turkey breast for Thanksgiving dinner. I thought it would be so much simpler than having to cook a turkey and a whole Thanksgiving meal out of our tiny oven. (How do they expect us to pull that off?) But apparently, the turkey breast I bought was actually a lump of non-sliced pressed turkey lunch meat! Saltiest turkey ever. Sad, sad, sad. At least the green bean casserole was good. HEY! I make a good green bean casserole for holiday meals! That should give me a little credit back.

We've had enchiladas for Christmas dinner before, too. But that was when I asked, "So what do you want to eat for Christmas dinner? A traditional turkey spread or something else?" And the reply was, "Enchiladas!" You can't blame me for that one!

One tradition we had for the years our sons were in college was a bad one. I'm such a sucker for giving presents too early. And my boys know that fact. And they use it to their advantage. The year of the Chinese buffet, the boys convinced me to let them open their presents five days before Christmas. "Mom, what difference does it make? It's just the four of us home this year. Why not just open our presents today? Why should we have to wait for a certain day to open our presents? That doesn't make sense. We can enjoy our gifts all week long." So they won. And it was fun. Our own, weird tradition of being un-traditional. Perhaps that counts as a tradition? Maybe that's our thing as a family.

I always thought that I would be the wife and mom

with glorious spreads of food, and decorated tables to rival anything Martha Stewart assembled. That just never happened. I found that I'm more of a paper-plate-buffet-line-in-the-kitchen kind of cook and entertainer. Perhaps because we had boys, and they really didn't care how fancy the table was decorated?

But I do love studying traditions. Particularly traditions that God's people remembered. And since this is a Bible study, let's see what God's word has to say about the importance of traditions, and why we keep them.

One of my all-time favorite portions of scripture is found in Joshua. It's not your typical 'favorite Joshua verse', but one that just happened to stick out to me personally. When Israel finally crossed into the Holy Land, across/through the Jordan river, God spoke to Joshua: "Select twelve men from the people, a man from each tribe, and tell them, 'From right here, the middle of the Jordan where the feet of the priests are standing firm, take twelve stones. Carry them across with you and set them down in the place where you camp tonight.'"

They did as God commanded, and then set up a 'stone altar' on the Holy Land bank of the Jordan. Then instructed, "Each of you heft a stone to your shoulder, a stone for each of the tribes of the People of Israel, so you'll have something later to mark the occasion. When your children ask you, 'What are these stones to you?' you'll say, 'The flow of the Jordan was stopped in front of the Chest of the Covenant of God as it crossed the Jordan—stopped in its tracks. These stones are a permanent memorial for the People of Israel.'" (Joshua chapter 4, verses 1-7)

I just absolutely love this portion of scripture. I love that God wanted those that witnessed his miracle to tell their children, and their children, and their children about what he did. Now that's the kind of tradition I want in my home! A 'memorial' of sorts. A physical reminder of what God has done for us, in the life of our family.

I can just imagine little Israelite children playing in the Jordan, and one asking, "Mom, what's that big pile of rocks for?", and the mother cuddling her child on her lap, and telling the amazing story of how God 'swept away' the mighty waters, and the whole nation of Israel walked across without getting a single drop of water on them. And every time they came to that spot hearing, "Mommy, tell me about those rocks, again, please!"

A tradition, where one verbally recalls God's power and miracles. I just love that. That's the kind of tradition worth keeping in your family.

For a long time (until her hands broke off), I kept one of those little Willow Tree angel figurines that held a '2006' in her hands. (In one of our recent moves, both hands (that had been previously re-glued with artificial nail glue) broke off for good, and got lost.) After reading the Joshua section about placing rocks to remember what God had done, I did the same sort of thing with that little angel. In 2006, God arranged a miracle for us to buy the house of our dreams. It was literally a miracle how it all transpired. I bought that figurine, and placed her right next to my kitchen sink, so that every time I rinsed or washed dishes in our sink, I would physically see a reminder of what God had done for our family in 2006. Instead of a huge pile of rocks, I decided a small angel would look a tad more appropriate in our kitchen.

Jewish family traditions, festivals, and feasts are so rich with meaning. I think we Christians that don't celebrate those symbolic Jewish times miss out a bit. I'm not telling you that we need to observe all of the rituals. I never did growing up, and we didn't with our boys, but the more I study them, the more beautiful and special they are.

The 'traditions' of observing the feasts are heavy with rich Godly symbolism. The Sabbath (God ordained day of rest, in Hebrew, called Shabbat), or Shabbat dinner begins with the lighting of candles to celebrate that God first created light. The blessing of the children comes next. Starting with the oldest, the parents will put their hands on the child's head and give the child a blessing. For both boys and girls, the rest of the blessing is:

May God bless you and guard you.
May God show you favor and be gracious to you.
May God show you kindness and grant you peace.

Most parents give each child a kiss after they are blessed. Now if you have ever watched the musical Fiddler On The Roof, you'll remember the song 'Sabbath Prayer', where Tevya (the father) and Golde (the mother) sing similar lyrics to their children. So beautiful. Such a deep, rich tradition to speak into the lives of children every Friday to children. I just looked that song up online, and I think I will be singing that song in my head all day long.

The symbolisms and traditions associated with the Shabbat dinner (and there are more than just the candle lighting and blessing of the children) are purposeful. Some family traditions are just for fun, and then there are the ones that are deeply meaningful. Don't get me wrong, I'm all about the fun ones, too. But those deeply meaningful God-inspired traditions hold something almost sacred.

Have you ever attended a Jewish Seder? It is the symbolic meal that takes place after sundown the night before the first official day of Passover. I have participated in a few Seders in my lifetime. The Seder is a ceremonial dinner that commemorates the Exodus from Egypt. During this dinner event, the Haggadah (the book containing the liturgy for the Seder service) is read, and the eating of symbolic foods is done. After the Seder service (it's kind of long), there is a big feast. But the Seder foods contain rich symbolism (including eating bitter herbs) pertaining to the hardships the Israelites endured at the hand of Egypt before being freed.

Here are the instructions that God, himself, laid out on how to 'celebrate' Passover. "And they shall take some of the blood (of a lamb or goat without blemish) and put it on the two doorposts and on the lintel of the houses where they eat it. Then they shall eat the flesh on that night; roasted in fire, with unleavened bread and with bitter herbs they shall eat it. Do not eat it raw, nor boiled at all with water, but roasted in fire; its head with its legs and its entrails. You shall let none of it remain until morning, and what remains of it until morning you shall burn with fire. And thus you shall eat it: with a belt on your waist, your sandals on your feet, and your staff in your hand. So you shall eat it in haste. It is the LORD's Passover." (Exodus 12:7-11)

And these are the instructions God gave for Israelites to observe every year at Passover time. I have learned that God is rather quite specific when it comes to how something should be done. There is always symbolism and distinct purpose to every instruction that God gives regarding biblical and Hebrew traditions to follow. There is always deeper meaning and significance involved.

I'm not trying to make your tradition of 'eating Christmas Chex mix while watching White Christmas' sound trivial. God is the one who instilled a love of traditions in us! He loves the 'do this in remembrance' stuff! I just think we need to balance out the fun/trivial "we do this every year" with a bit of deeper symbolism of what "God has done in our lives" activities. I'm completely not belittling the fun family traditions. Just throw a little spiritual balance in there. And I'm not suggesting that this Christmas you slaughter an unblemished lamb, and spread the blood over your front door. (Or at Easter for that matter)

Perhaps there are certain Christmas tree ornaments that remind you of times when God has interceded, or blessed you. I have seen 'Our First Year' or 'Baby's First Christmas' ornaments. When you hang those particular ornaments, you can take a few moments to verbally remember how God worked to bring the two of you together, or share with your child as he or she gets older, what a miracle it was to have them come into your life. What a blessing, as you hang those 'first year' ornaments, to share with your family times of blessings and remembrances.

Our first married Christmas, I sewed together heart shaped and stuffed plaid Christmas ornaments. They weren't fancy. They weren't store-bought. They were extremely simple. But every time I view them on our tree, it reminds me of the tremendous blessings we've experienced in our family since that first Christmas. It also reminds me of how blessed I am to live another year with my amazing husband. Those are great traditions to remember and 'celebrate'.

Four years ago, my husband and I had the honor of traveling to Israel. In Bethlehem, there are dozens of shops where you can purchase anything and everything olive wood. We purchased these mini-sized olive wood Christmas ornaments. I was so excited to decorate our tree that year with our Bethlehem-memory ornaments. But once Christmas rolled around, I had completely forgotten about them. They were in a still unpacked bag from the trip, which I re-discovered just last year when we were moving. How sad is that?

Here were these wonderful reminders from the actual town Jesus was born in, sitting in our storage area, completely unpacked—along with tourist brochures, and placemats from the Sea of Galilee. See. I told you I wasn't the best at keeping traditions!

I pinkie promise that from this year on, we will use those ornaments, and chat about how God moved throughout that amazing trip to the Holy Land. Unfortunately, I won't be using the Sea of Galilee placemats, because some Israeli hotel shampoos (that somehow were also in that forgotten bag) spilled all over the placemats. Ladies and gentlemen, spilled shampoo over time turns moldy.

Psalm 34 verse 8 tells us to "Taste and see that the LORD is good; blessed is the one who takes refuge in him." Some people have this verse stenciled on their kitchen walls, or on crafty plaques. I do love this verse. It's a wonderful reminder in the season when we tend to gorge ourselves on turkey, stuffing, green bean casserole, pies, and cookies. In the midst of all our Christmas partying, eating, and festivities, it is because of the Lord's goodness in our lives that we are able to feast, and enjoy special times with our loved ones.

This Christmas season, may you indeed 'Taste and see that the Lord is good'. And as you keep old traditions passed down from generation to generation, and instill new ones, may they be beautiful reminders of God's goodness and faithfulness.

- Psalm 78: 3-6
- 2 Thess 2:15
- 1 Corinthians 15: 1-5

Chat Time

What is your favorite childhood Christmas tradition? Why was it so special?

What is your favorite family tradition now? Why is it your favorite now? Who decided that this would be a tradition in your family?

Do you heavily rely on family traditions, or are you one to make up your own, new ones? If so, what new ones have you incorporated into your family life?

What is your typical Christmas day like? What do you traditionally eat? Do you hand out presents? Any traditional way that your family goes about opening the presents?

Do you have a favorite Christmas tree ornament? Why is it special and different from the others? What memories or feelings does it bring?

I always loved Christmas Eve candle light services. What is your favorite Christmas church event? Why? Is your family involved? What makes it different from other church events or services? Does your church have a Christmas Eve service? Do you attend it?

chat christmas

Have you ever done something just for 'tradition sake', and later regretted it, because you knew your heart really wasn't in it? Are there some traditions, that in your opinion need to be done away with? What are they?

Is there a tradition from your husband's side of the family that you loved, and incorporated into your own? Is there one from his side, that you *don't* like, and would rather drop?

How open was your husband to incorporating Christmas traditions that were perhaps different from ones he was used to, but you wanted to keep?

What are the top significant things that God has done in your life? How do you remember them? Have you ever bought or built something in order to remind yourself of what he has done for you?

Do you tell your children about the miracles God has performed in your life? What are your favorite 'miracle stories' that you share with your loved ones? What can you personally do to never daily forget what he has done?

Do you (*come on, be honest*) remember to say a 'grace' before every meal? Are families getting away from that? Why do you think we say 'grace'? Is it biblical? Did Jesus tell us to do that?

What family traditions have you seen other families keep, that you would like to incorporate into your family? Why?

Have you ever participated in a Passover Seder? How did it make you feel? Is it something your church traditionally participates in? Why do you believe God instituted this yearly meal/ritual for his people? Are we Evangelical Christians supposed to follow suit, and observe a Seder meal? Did Jesus observe the Passover? Do you have any Jewish friends? Did you know any Jewish people while you were growing up? Do/did they observe a traditional Sabbath?

Should we, Christians, be following the strict God-given traditions of a Sabbath? Why don't we? Was it just meant for Jewish people? Is there a Bible verse that released people from following a Sabbath? Why do you think God instituted the strict Sabbath rules? Have you ever attended a Shabbat dinner? What was it like? What made it special or different from other dinners?

What's the difference between a biblical tradition and a biblical *law*? Are we required to observe both? Are there New Testament scriptures that release us of following the traditions and rituals God set forth for his people to observe? Why don't Christians stick to a strict Sabbath law? Did Jesus observe the Sabbath?

chat christmas

Should Christians still keep the Passover? Why should or shouldn't we? If we are 'God's people' under the new covenant, doesn't that still include all of the rituals God ordained for his children to follow?

What is the importance of tradition? Is it important to keep traditions? What percent of people do you think observe certain Christmas traditions without really knowing the significance behind it?

Even non-believers celebrate Christmas. Is this right or wrong? Why would someone who doesn't have a personal relationship with Jesus celebrate his birth? Or is Christmas just thought of as a fun holiday? Should they be 'allowed' to celebrate Christmas?

Do your family holiday traditions give you a sense of belonging? How?

Because traditions are familiar, you know what to expect because the tradition has been repeated over time. There is no surprise or anything new. You have fond memories of the last time you participated and you feel a sense of security. Is this the "why" of why we keep traditions alive? Are there some traditions that have become so 'familiar', that they have lost their significance over time?

Ending Thought

I actually like the feel of fun family and also deeply spiritual Christmas time traditions. I just don't want to be one that observes traditions *simply* for tradition sake. When there is meaning and significance behind a tradition, it makes it a symbol of importance and remembrance. That's why I love the story of God telling Joshua to take the stones out of the Jordan when they crossed. 'So that you can tell your children what God did for you today'.

Perhaps in the midst of the fun traditions, or driving around the neighborhoods to see the Christmas light displays, you can tell those with you how many miracles the Lord 'performed' for you this past year. And as you nibble on cookies and cocoa, share with your loved ones and especially the children in the family, how blessed they are to have tasty goodies, and that God is the one who provides those blessings to us.

Keep the traditions? Sure! Just keep God smack dab in the middle of all of them!

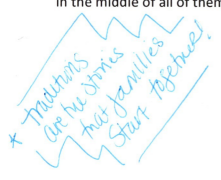

* Traditions are the stories that families start together.

Family Scriptures

* 1 Corinthians 13:4-7
* 1 John 4:19
* Acts 10:2
* Acts 16:31-34
* Ephesians 3:14-15
* 2 Timothy 1:5
* Colossians 3:13

it's all relative(s)

OK, so it's not the most original title. It's been used before. But nothing else seemed to fit. So much of the holiday exhaustion is dealing with relatives. Did I just say *dealing* as if it were something difficult to do? Surely not. I meant that we *get* to be around our extended family during this season.

I always love to give illustrations from my own life when I write. But I think you'll agree with me, that this might not be the wisest choice, when writing a chapter about getting along with relatives! So, bear with me as I use wording like them/they/'you people', etc. Secretly, I *may* or may *not* be referring to people I personally know. Perhaps I should have waited to write this chapter until anyone that I *may* be referring to is in Heaven. But then you have that whole 'great cloud of witnesses' situation to deal with. Can they *really* watch us from up there, and hear what we say or write about them?

See my point about writing this chapter? I'm only in my first of many paragraphs, and it's a sticky situation. Gulp.

Recently a physician remarked on a new patient's extraordinarily ruddy complexion, he said, "High blood pressure, Doc. It comes from my family." "Your mother's side or your father's?" the doctor asked. "Neither," he replied, "it's from my wife's family." "Oh, come now. How could your wife's family give you high blood pressure?" he sighed. "You oughta meet 'em sometime, Doc!"

Joke. That's just a *joke*. Remember, this chapter isn't about anyone in *my* family. Perhaps some of you have difficult family members you have to deal with from time to time. Perhaps it is an in-law that is tough to be around or an aunt or uncle who is difficult to get along with. If I were to ask you, "Who is the most difficult member in your family?" immediately, someone will likely come to mind.

Christmas is often referred to as 'The Most Wonderful Time Of The Year'. And well, in so many ways it is. I love Christmas and all of its festivities and food. Cozy fires, sipping hot chocolate, singing Christmas carols, watching ELF, and decorating the Christmas tree are all some of my favorite activities of the season. The children's eyes full of wonder and anticipation. My mother reminding me to wash my hands before I eat dinner (did I just write that?).

We all have a different family history. No two alike. Even for siblings, each has different memories. An older sibling may remember their childhood as a completely different experience from the baby in the family. Some have great memories. Some have such extreme sadness. Perhaps Christmas is a time that reminds you that your parents are no longer together, and the image of the perfect family you always wanted was shattered. Or perhaps there is an emptiness from loved ones that are no longer with us to celebrate this season.

Whatever the past, we have to face our present. And if you are the one with a perfect set of parents, siblings, and the picture perfect in-laws, then perhaps you can go ahead and prepare snack time for the group. Cause the rest of us may need to work through a few things. Myself included.

In my research for writing this particular chapter, I thought I would find oodles of Bible verses proving my hypothesis. That it's wiser and just easier not to spend time around difficult family members. Don't like 'em, or want to spend time around 'em? No worries. The Bible will tell us that we can just ignore those we don't get along with. Unfortunately, I didn't find a lot of verses with that frame of thought. But I did find some passages that let us know we are not alone.

Do you have that one sibling that is always trying to get to you? To push your buttons? If you do, you're not the only one. What I love about God's word, is that he is gracious enough to give us biblical examples that show us that others have walked through similar scenarios.

Young David was about to face off with Goliath. I'm

not exactly sure how old David was when he fought the giant. Probably a young teenager. So here is David, about to take on the battle of his life, mustering up all the God-courage he can, when his *brother* (in front of everyone) verbally cuts him down!

David was talking with other soldiers about what would happen to the man who killed Goliath, when "Eliab, David's oldest brother, heard him speaking with the men, he burned with anger at him and asked, 'Why have you come down here? And with whom did you leave those few sheep in the wilderness? I know how conceited you are and how wicked your heart is; you came down only to watch the battle.'" (I Samuel 17:28)

Talk about ugly words and jealousy. And from David's oldest *brother*! His own flesh and blood. Why is it that some of the harshest words come from the ones we love? David's oldest brother should have either been so incredibly proud of his brother's bold braveness, or tried to protect and shelter him. But instead, he calls him conceited and *wicked*. Wow. Crazy thing is, we don't hear much more about Eliab. But we do about David. Because, even with the ugly words his brother said, God chose to work through him, and we know that David (even with his faults) was 'a man after God's own heart'.

Thankfully, David didn't let those mean words affect him to the point that he couldn't accomplish what God ordained for him to do. The same holds true for you. God has his hand on your life, and knows the future he has for you. You can't let (I know, *easier said than done*) the hostile words of a relative affect the calling he has for your life. That's what sometimes makes this Christmas season tricky in regards to relationships and time spent together with family. Often, those who know us best, are the ones who can hurt us the deepest.

I really don't mean to be a Debbie Downer by having a Christmas Bible Study go in this direction. I'm just trying to keep it real. Shall we continue?

So how do you respond to that relative or person that verbally attacks you? Do you isolate yourself from them? Refuse to speak to them? Are you embarrassed by them? Could the person you see as being the most difficult member in your family actually become an opportunity to minister the loving presence of the Lord Jesus Christ?

Every Christian should make loving their family priority, even those who are a bit rough around the edges. Not easy. Not necessarily fun. If this seems impossible right now to you, I completely understand. Dealing with difficult people not only tests our faith in God, but it also puts our witness on display. Me? I'd rather just not invite them. That option just seems easier. But it doesn't always work that way.

Later on in King David's life, the Amalekites had attacked the village of Ziklag, carrying off the wives and children of David's army men. Scripture says David and his men wept until they had no strength left. Understandably the men were angry, but instead of being mad at the Amalekites, they blamed David: "David was greatly distressed because the men were talking of stoning him; each was bitter in spirit because of his sons and daughters." (1 Samuel 30:6, NIV)

Often people take their anger out on us. Sometimes we deserve it, in which case an apology is needed, but usually the difficult person is frustrated in general and we are the handiest target. Striking back is not the solution: "But David strengthened himself in the LORD his God." (1 Samuel 30:6) David ended up bringing every single person back that had been abducted. David didn't return the harsh words with slanderous remarks. Instead he sought the Lord's guidance, and God gave him the answers he needed. I hope those guys apologized to David!

Turning to God when we're attacked by an angry person gives us understanding, patience, and most of all, courage. Some suggest taking a deep breath or counting to ten, but the real answer is saying a quick prayer. David asked God what to do, was told to pursue the kidnappers, and he and his men rescued their families. God provided the answer to David's difficult situation with those who 'had it out' for him.

Another solution is walking away. Sometimes you honestly can't rationalize with a person. And I think making some space, and 'taking a breather' is healthy. We can't control difficult people and we can't change them, but with God's guidance we can attempt to understand them better and find a way to cope with them. *If* from a distance, if we need to.

Even Jesus taught his disciples, right before they were headed out on their own to minister, that it was

chat christmas

OK to leave, if they were not welcomed by someone. "Jesus now called the Twelve and gave them authority and power to deal with all the demons and cure diseases. He commissioned them to preach the news of God's kingdom and heal the sick. He said, 'Don't load yourselves up with equipment. Keep it simple; you are the equipment. And no luxury inns—get a modest place and be content there until you leave. If you're not welcomed, leave town. Don't make a scene. Shrug your shoulders and move on.'" (Luke 9:1-5)

Another version of that text says that Jesus told the disciples to "shake the dust off their feet". This is an Eastern idiom, meaning you need to shake off any animosity or bitterness that you may have toward someone. So that when you leave, you leave in peace and with no regrets, anger, blame or hurt. "Shaking the dust off your feet" means that you don't carry any of that with you. You leave it all there and go on your way.

So in other words, you *won't* always be welcomed— even with those that are guests in *your* home. Sometimes it's perfectly fine to 'shrug your shoulders and move on'. Often times that's the safest way to handle difficult people. But what if you're stuck? What if your in-laws booked their return flight three weeks after their arrival, and they're *there* for a long time?

Perhaps this verse will give you some wisdom, "Proverbs 22:3, A prudent man foresees evil and hides himself". Come on, that's funny, no? Perhaps I just slightly took that verse out of context, but ya gotta admit, it's a good one. *Evil* relatives? *Never.* (But maybe there is some truth in that verse?) Could a person stay hidden in their room for a full three weeks?

But honestly, how to you make it through a potentially trying time, when you have those long-term guests that seem to get under your skin? This is a great verse, "He who has knowledge spares his words, and a man of understanding is of a calm spirit. Even a fool is counted wise when he holds his peace; when he shuts his lips, he is considered perceptive." (Proverbs 17:27-28) That's great wisdom. It's not easy to do *at all* sometimes, but it's so worth it for personal mental survival! 'Spare your words, and keep calm'. Remember, they *will* be going home, and life will return to normal eventually.

Perhaps you are the parent, and your adult children and their families are coming to visit. The Proverbs 17 verse still holds true. No adult child wants instruction from their parents. Especially in front of their spouse and children. That parent-adult child relationship can be tricky.

The last time I checked, this verse was still true, "For this cause a man shall leave his father and his mother, and shall cleave (cling to) to his wife" (Genesis 2:24). We (myself included) parents that have married children need to remember that we have a different relationship with them now. We're not responsible for them anymore. Their spouse is. If you look at it from the proper angle, it could be a great 'relief'. You've done your job. The bell on the oven rang, and they're 'cooked'. Done. Finished. Cut the apron strings, and enjoy your child as a full-fledged co-adult in this world.

I think, that when you let them go, and aren't constantly reminding them to still make their bed, and hang up their towels, that it's a freedom. What *wife* wants to hear their Mother-in-Law reminding her husband to 'pick up your underwear'? He's a big boy now.

Ladies, have you ever had an argument/fight with your husband, when you had relatives in the house? It's the worst. You have to thoroughly express yourself to him with a *strong* whisper and heavily rely on facial expressions to make your point known, and that's not an easy thing to do. You feel like your guests are listening to everything. Trying to hear you. Yet, when you walk out of the doors of your bedroom, you have to be all smiles, acting as if everything between you and your hubby *couldn't be better*. Such weird games we play for emotional survival!

Is it wrong to admit that there are some Bible verses I'm not so fond of? One's that make you realize just how far off you are sometimes? Proverbs 17:27-28 is one of those passages. "He that has knowledge spares his words: and a man of understanding is of an excellent spirit. Even a fool, when he holds his peace, is counted wise: and he that shuts his lips is esteemed a man of understanding." I *could* simply write this entire section off, because it has the word *man* in it. Not woman. But I know better. I don't really like to 'spare my words'. And 'holding peace' when you *know* someone else was completely wrong with their words or actions is sincerely hard for me. But Christmas *is* a season of peace. Peace. *Wonderful peace---coming down from the Father above.*

I'm sure there may be some of you reading this chapter that honestly don't run into any of these family and extended family situations. And if so, I think that's wonderful. Maybe something in this chapter will come to your mind down the road, if there's ever a 'situation' you have to deal with. And for those of us who can relate to what I've written, I pray that this holiday (Thanksgiving thru Christmas) season will be one of peace and refreshing.

There are so many wonderful times that we all experience with loved ones at this special time of year. I most certainly don't want to belittle the joy of having loved ones gather together to remember and celebrate the birth of our Lord. Wonderful memories of cousins playing together. Opening presents from parents. Giving presents to those we love. Having our grown children back under our roof. Those are the experiences we need to concentrate on, as we walk through the seasons of Thanksgiving and Christmas. Some of the loved ones gathered in our family rooms this year, may not be with us next year. That's why it's so important to do our best to *make it work* with joy and peace. To the best of our abilities.

May you take deep breaths, and enjoy the beauty of this special time of year. May you not get so overwhelmed with parties, gatherings, family squabbles, and church events that you miss out on the spirit of why we celebrate a time of giving thanks, and the season to celebrate the greatest gift this world ever received.

Chat Time

Only do this if you *don't* have a relative in your small group that will get upset---but share your craziest situation with family/guests over the holidays. Funniest? Hardest? Most frustrating? What was said/done? How did the situation get resolved?

Have you ever had to 'agree to disagree' with a family member? What was the situation about? How did the 'agree to disagree' conversation go? What was the end result? Did the 'agreement' hold? Was it hard for you to keep that agreement?

Why do you think tensions rise around the holidays?

Are you a 'busier is better' type holiday person, or do you like to chill, and kick back during this time of year?

Let's say your Mother-in-Law just told your husband that they are planning on staying with you for a lot longer than originally expected. You know that this would not be a good scenario for your family. Do you take a deep breath, and say, 'OK, fine.' Or do you tell your husband they need to change their plans? Would your husband support what *you* feel is right in this scenario, or could he *not* tell his parents, "no"?

What is your favorite 'get through this' Bible verse? What helps you re-focus on God during tough times? What is your personal secret to 'keeping your cool'?

I Peter 4:4-6 tells us, "Of course, your old friends don't understand why you don't join in with the old gang anymore. But you don't have to give an account to them. They're the ones who will be called on the carpet—and before God himself."

Sometimes family members are upset with you *because* of your faith. Perhaps you are the single one who became a Christian, and they are at odds with you because of that. The above verse tells us that 'your old friends don't understand why you don't join in….'. Has there ever been a time in your life when your family was at odds with you because of your faith? How did you handle it? What was said? How do you, personally handle Christmas time with the non-believer in your family? Are they simply tolerant of you? Are you tolerant of them? Does it cause a distance between you? Why do you think they feel the way they do about you?

Have you ever had a family member tell you that your religion was a 'crutch'? How did you respond? How do you confront people like that? How did it make you feel?

Proverbs 17:27-28, "He who has knowledge spares his

words, and a man of understanding is of a calm spirit. Even a fool is counted wise when he holds his peace; when he shuts his lips, he is considered perceptive."

On a scale from 1-10, how good are you with 'sparing your words' with difficult family members? Can you recall a time when you *didn't* spare your words? What were the circumstances? How did it turn out? How about a time when you *did* spare your words. What difference did it make in you? In them?

The Bible tells us to 'Honor your father and mother', but how does one do that, when they lie, or do wrong to us?

Proverbs 16:7 tells us, "When a man's ways please the Lord, he makes even his enemies to be at peace with him." Does this sound too good to be true? Have you seen a change in 'enemies' towards you when you have tried to 'please the Lord'. Or do you think 'haters are just going to hate' no matter what? Share an example of either school of thought.

"Make no friendship with an angry man, and with a furious man do not go, lest you learn his ways and set a snare for your soul." (Proverbs 22:24-25) What if it's someone in your *family* that is the 'angry man'? How do you interpret this verse in that scenario? Do you set boundaries? What kind of boundaries or restraints do you set with this 'angry man/woman'? Have you had to do this with your own family? How did it work out?

"Therefore, my beloved brethren, let every man be swift to hear, slow to speak, slow to anger: For the anger of man does not produce the righteousness of God." (James 1:19-20) This verse is *so* against my nature. I'm ready to 'duke it out'. No slowness. Bring it on. I kinda really don't like this verse, to be honest. Especially if I know I'm right, and they're wrong.

Convince me that I'm wrong. Tell the group a time when you heeded these words, and it changed the atmosphere of your discussion/fight. Are you like me, you like to fight/talk it out right away at full force, or are you one that can easily walk away, and resolve issues at another time, after you have taken time to 'think about it'?

"Death and life are in the power of the tongue: and they that love it shall eat the fruit thereof." (Proverbs 18:21) Have you ever said something in anger to someone, and figuratively saw 'the life go out' of them? Has that ever happened to you? Give an example of when words negatively affected your spirit, then balance it out with an example of when someone 'spoke life' into your soul.

Ending Thought

Romans 12:18 tells us, "If it is possible, as far as it depends on you, live at peace with everyone". Easier said than done at times. Especially with extended family members. It's odd to me that sometimes those who grow up in the same household can be such polar opposites in their adult lives.

God's word is black and white when it comes to how we should respect and get along with one another. The old song *'And they'll know we are Christians by our love, by our love. Yes, they'll know we are Christians by our love'* speaks a simplistic message. Remember the song? That chorus often comes to mind when dealing with difficult people. God knew it wouldn't be easy. I believe that's why he gave us so many scriptures to help us along this journey of family relationships.

And to think that one of most joyous season of the year can also be one of the toughest, in regards to getting along with everyone. I pray that *this* will be the year of peace and deep joy with all of your relatives.

If all fails, remember—January is just around the corner.

inn keeping

Most every Christmas pageant or Christmas musical has one. He's (or *she's*—if you're an edgy, cutting edge type of church) an integral character in the Christmas story. The Inn Keeper. Over forty-eight years of hearing, seeing, and singing in Christmas musicals and dramas, I have come to the conclusion that we Americans interpret the infamous Inn Keeper two ways. There is the overly exhausted, grumpy, grouchy, not very helpful, keeper that pretty much dismisses Joseph and Mary. Then there is the kind, tender hearted Inn Keeper, that would *love* to provide a room for Mary to give birth in, but unfortunately there simply just is "...no room..." There are even sermons and songs *about* the inn keeper! How he felt, how we should or shouldn't be *like* the inn keeper in the Bible.

A few years ago, my husband and I were privileged to have that dream trip to the Holy Land. Honestly, we never thought that was a trip we would be able to take, but we went with a ministry that paid for us to go. (A miracle!) We got to tour much of the country, and when we were in Jerusalem, we had a day trip down to Bethlehem. Honestly, going into Bethlehem was a tad scary. The town is now located in the West Bank, and doesn't feel very safe. Big difference in feeling from Jerusalem. As we were driving through the roads in Bethlehem on our tour bus, we could see military men armed with machine guns. We had a Palestinian tour guide for that day, and my husband asked him, "Where was the inn where Joseph and Mary tried to get a room?"

I distinctly remember the look on the tour guide's face. It was total, "Huh? What are you talking about?" He had no idea what my husband was asking, and dismissed the question. We toured the Church of the Nativity (that has the supposed birth place of Jesus underneath it). Very cool. Very old. Still a lot of machine-gun-toting men outside the church. Gave me the heebie jeebies. I was ready to get back to 'safe' Jerusalem. But I didn't forget how oddly the tour guide responded to Dave's question about the Inn Keeper.

The next day, we toured the Garden Tomb (one of the presumed burial spots of Jesus). While walking the garden, I noticed these large brown 'pods' that had fallen from the trees. I love plants and gardening, and asked him what those pods were. He said, "Those are locust tree pods. That's what John the Baptist ate. He would grind up the seeds in the pods, and mix it with honey. The seeds taste similar to chocolate when ground up."

Locust pods? Locust *trees*? *"The guminous evergreen tree (Ceratonia siliqua) native to the E Mediterranean region and cultivated elsewhere. The pods and their extracted content have numerous common names, e.g., locust bean gum, or "Saint John's Bread", in the belief that the "locusts" on which John the Baptist fed were carob pods. The tree, about 50 ft. (15 m) tall, bears compound, glossy leaves with thick leaflets. Its red flowers are followed by flat, leathery pods that contain 5-15 hard brown seeds embedded in a sweet, edible pulp that tastes similar to chocolate."* -- The Columbia Encyclopedia, 6th Edition. Copyright © 2002 Columbia University Press

STOP THE BUS! John the Baptist *didn't* eat locust *BUGS*?! Ever since I can remember---in every Sunday school booklet, and on every felt board demonstration, John the Baptist was portrayed as a whacked out *bug eater.* There was always a bit of an "euwwww" feeling when it came to John the Baptist. I pictured him as a dreadlock wearing, leather-hide-loin-cloth-sporting, crazed cousin of Jesus. And now I learned that he had a sweet tooth, and make a concoction of *chocolate-flavored* carob seeds and honey! He was a candy maker! Shut the front door!

The whole non-locust bug revelation in Israel made me re-think the Inn Keeper question my husband asked the Palestinian tour guide. He had seemed extremely knowledgeable about everything else about Bethlehem, besides the inn question. What if we

Americans were wrong about the Inn Keeper, as we had been about John the Baptist's daily diet of insects? What if there (gasp!) wasn't actually an *inn*? What if the Christmas story I had believed my whole life was actually just a misinterpretation of scripture (like the *locust*)?

So I started digging and researching. I read through all of the gospel accounts of the birth of Jesus, and to my surprise, I did not find one single verse that mentions an inn keeper.

"And it came to pass in those days, that there went out a decree from Caesar Augustus that all the world should be taxed. And this taxing was first made when Cyrenius was governor of Syria. And all went to be taxed, every one into his own city. And Joseph also went up from Galilee, out of the city of Nazareth, into Judaea, unto the city of David, which is called Bethlehem; (because he was of the house and lineage of David); To be taxed with Mary his espoused wife, being great with child. And so it was, that, while they were there, the days were accomplished that she should be delivered. And she brought forth her firstborn son, and wrapped him in swaddling clothes, and laid him in a manger; because there was no room for them in the inn." Luke 2: 1-7

The book of Matthew does not mention anything about an inn, or specific details about the birth of Jesus. The gospels of John and Mark don't even start out with an account of the birth of Jesus. Matthew is focused more on the wise men going to Herod and visiting Jesus. Luke is our single portrayal of the typical Bethlehem inn/manger/no room event. There is only one telling of that account. So why didn't the tour guide understand this hotel concept? If they had documented the area Jesus was born in, wouldn't an ancient inn/hotel be right next to it? What happened to *that* structure?

I started doing a little research and digging. This was suddenly fascinating to me. What if. What *if* how we portray how Jesus came into this world—just Joseph and Mary in a lowly stable, by themselves—is actually a *false* retelling of what happened that night? Had we made the story so 'American' that we assumed the word 'inn' (from the King James version) literally meant 'hotel/motel'?

The original language Luke was written in was Greek, so I thought it appropriate to see what the Greek word for inn actually was. The Word used in the original writing of Luke for the account of Jesus' birth was the word *kataluma*. Kataluma means a place of rest, usually a guest room. In fact, the same writer Luke uses this very word later where it clearly refers to a guest room and not an inn. Notice Luke:22:11, where Jesus said to his disciples, "Then you shall say to the master of the house, The Teacher says to you, "'Where is the guest room [kataluma] where I may eat the Passover with My disciples?" The *upper room* where Jesus held His last supper was the same word 'inn'/kataluma. It's so interesting to me what can happen to words when they are translated into different languages.

Luke elsewhere in his Gospel uses a different Greek word when he writes about an actual inn—not the word kataluma. In the parable of the Good Samaritan, Jesus mentions that the injured man in the story was taken to an inn—and here Luke translates using the Greek word *pandokheion*, the normal word for an inn. We read this in Luke:10:34, where the kind Samaritan set the injured man "on his own animal, brought him to an inn, and took care of him." If, indeed, there had been no room for Mary and Joseph in the well know Inn Keeper-inn, the word used there in the original Greek would have been *pandokheion*.

To further dig into this mystery about how we currently view the birth of Christ, it is 'allowed' to look into the culture of the times, and what it would have been like back when Joseph returned to his ancestral home in Bethlehem. Remember that *all* of Joseph's family were to return there, to be counted for in this huge census. Joseph, and however many brothers, sisters, cousins, aunts, and uncles would have also been in Bethlehem at that time.

In Christ's day, hospitality to visitors among the Jews was essential, based on biblical example and law. In Deuteronomy 10:19, God told the Israelites to "love the stranger." And Leviticus 19:33 states, "If a stranger dwells with you in your land, you shall not mistreat him." Denial of hospitality was shown throughout scripture to be an outrage. Hospitality toward visitors is still important throughout the Middle East.

Since Joseph was a descendant of King David, whose hometown this was, he would have been highly respected upon his arrival. Think of a descendant of George Washington coming to his hometown of Alexandria, Virginia, after a long lapse of time. The townspeople would've shown him respect.

It should also be pointed out that childbirth was a major event at that time. In a small village like Bethlehem, many neighboring women would have come to help in the birth. In the case of a birth, the men will sit apart with the neighbors, but the room will be full of women assisting the midwife. A private home would have bedding, facilities for heating water and all that is required for any normal birth.

What this all means is that it would have been unthinkable and an unimaginable insult and affront to societal decency for Joseph, a returning village son, and his laboring wife to need to seek shelter in an unsavory inn to have a baby of Davidic descent—and then, even worse, to be sent out to have the birth in a stable.

Are you still with me? Hang in there. Just a bit more.

Careful reading of the text shows us they had already been in Bethlehem for some days when she went into labor. Notice carefully Luke:2:4-6, "Joseph also went up from Galilee, out of the city of Nazareth into Judea, to the city of David, which is called Bethlehem, because he was of the house and lineage of David, to be registered with Mary, his betrothed wife, who was with child. So it was, that *while they were there*, the days were completed for her to be delivered."

So Joseph and Mary didn't come riding into Bethlehem *last minute* frantically looking for a motel room so that Mary could give birth. They had already *been* there.

There? Well, where were they staying? We don't have literal Biblical wording proof of where they stayed during their time in Bethlehem. But, in keeping with Israeli traditions at that time, they were probably staying in the family home in Bethlehem. If Joseph's family all had to get together and be in one place in order to be counted for the census, the house would be full of people! The upper chamber room (kataluma) would have gone to the respected elders in the family. Bethlehem is extremely mountainous, and the houses are built on the sides of hills/mountains, and they have many levels.

Eric F.F. Bishop, an expert in Middle East culture, noted that the birth of Christ probably took place in "one of the Bethlehem houses with the lower section provided for the animals, with mangers 'hollowed in stone,' the dais (or raised area) being reserved for the family. Such a manger being immovable, filled with crushed straw, would do duty for a cradle. An infant might even be left in safety, especially if swaddled, when the mother was absent on temporary business".

Agricultural equipment, olive oil, wine, wheat, grains, milk, etc. were all kept down in the lower level of the home. The prized animals were usually taken indoors at night, so that thieves could not steal them. Having the animals in the lower level, actually provided warmth for the upper levels, and the use of animal dung as warming fuel was another reason to have the animals inside.

The 'family room' in homes, often was a terraced area above where the animals were kept. So here is a new picture. Joseph and Mary made it to Bethlehem. They are staying in a family home (presumably one of Joseph's relatives).

The upper room/kataluma/inn/guest room was already filled with the elderly in the family who had come because of the census. Joseph and Mary were surrounded with family. When it came time for Mary to deliver, she was probably surrounded by the women and mid-wives in Joseph's family. Baby Jesus, because of crowding, was placed in the animal's manger. It was a nice, safe, environment for him, and very typical of what would normally take place in a Hebrew family home.

And just one more interesting tidbit I have to include. You *do* know that the probability of Jesus being born on the exact date of December 25th is possibly wrong, right? Despite the infamous t-shirt, tree ornament, Christmas cards, and wall plaque saying that tells is that 'Jesus Is The Reason For The Season'. The season in which we celebrate Christ's birth has pagan roots.

Pagans celebrated a festival involving a heroic supernatural figure that visits an evergreen tree and leaves gifts on December 25th long before Jesus was ever born.   From its early Babylonian roots, the celebration of the birth or "rebirth" of the sun god on December 25th came to be celebrated under various names all over the ancient world. The winter solstice occurs a few days before December 25th each year. The winter solstice is the day of the year when daylight is the shortest. In ancient times, December 25th was the day each year when the day started to become noticeably longer. Therefore it was fitting for the early pagans to designate December 25th as the date of the birth or the "rebirth" of the sun.

The word for Christmas in late Old English is Cristes Maesse, the Mass of Christ, first found in 1038. By the time the Roman Empire legalized Christianity in the 4th century, most of the other religions in the empire were celebrating the birth of their gods on December 25th.

Leading up to December 25th in ancient Rome, a festival known as Saturnalia was one of the biggest celebrations of the year. Saturnalia was a festival during which the Romans commemorated the dedication of the temple of their god Saturn. This holiday began on the 17th of December and it would last for an entire week until the 23rd of December.

Saturnalia was typically characterized by gift-giving, feasting, singing and lots and lots of debauchery. The priests of Saturn would carry wreaths of evergreen boughs in procession throughout the pagan Roman temples.

In the year 350 A.D., Pope Julius I declared that the birth of Jesus would be celebrated on December 25th from then on. There appears to be little doubt that Pope Julius was trying to make it as painless as possible for pagan Romans to convert to Catholicism.

The Bible does not specifically say the date of Jesus' birth. We know it was not during the winter months because the sheep were in the pasture (Luke 2:8). A study of the time of the conception of John the Baptist reveals he was possibly conceived about Sivan 30, the eleventh week (Torah's calendar).

When Zechariah was ministering in the temple, he received an announcement from God of a coming son. The 'eighth course of Abia', when Zechariah was ministering, was the week of Sivan 12 to 18 (Killian n.d.). Adding forty weeks for a normal pregnancy reveals that John the Baptist was born on or about Passover (Nisan 14). We know six months after John's conception, Mary conceived Jesus (Luke 1:26-33). Therefore, Jesus would have been conceived six months later in the month of Kislev. Kislev 25 is Hanukkah. Was the "light of the world" conceived on the festival of lights?

Starting at Hanukkah, which begins on Kislev 25 and continues for eight days, and counting through the nine months of Mary's pregnancy, one arrives at the approximate time of the birth of Jesus at the Festival of Tabernacles (the early fall of the year).

The Hebrew word for "feasts" (moadim) literally means "appointed times." God has carefully planned and orchestrated the timing and sequence of each of these seven feasts to reveal to us a special story. How God-like would it be for Jesus, The Light of The World, to be conceived during Hanukkah, and then to be born during the Feast of Tabernacles, which is a feast of joy and celebration that God abided *with* them.

To *me* the dates and significance of those probable dates and times makes a *whole lot* more sense than combining the celebration of Jesus' birth with that of a pagan god's time of 'debauchery'.

Why this chapter? To study and know truth. I love Christmas, and all its beautiful symbolism. I'm not trying to be a Christmas Grinch! Study, study, study. Know, know, know. And if this chapter bothers you, feel free to tear it out. But I hope at least, that I have planted a mustard seed of desire to seek out the truth. Come to your *own* conclusion about what happened to Mary and Joseph in Bethlehem. Dig to see if there is more symbolism to the actual birth time of Jesus, rather than just a date set to bring more people into the church.

Merry Christmas!

Chat Time

Is reading this chapter more disturbing, or interesting to you?

Did you always believe that John the Baptist literally ate locust insects? Were you as surprised as I was? Had you ever heard of the 'locust pod' in reference to what John the Baptist ate? Why do you think people misinterpreted the 'locust' that John the Baptist ate?

Are you upset that Kirsten questioned the typical version we were taught of the Christmas story? Have you *not* questioned what you were raised to believe according the Inn Keeper and that Mary and Joseph did not have anywhere to stay upon arrival in Bethlehem---and believe what is in this chapter is perhaps heresy?

What did Mary ride into Bethlehem? What does the scripture say about her mode of transportation? Can you give the specific verse?

Is it OK to question what you have always been taught?

Acts 17:11 states, "Now the Berean Jews were of more noble character than those in Thessalonica, for they received the message with great eagerness and examined the Scriptures every day to see if what Paul said was true." What does this scripture mean to you? Do you examine scriptures to make sure they are true? How *does* one go about examining scriptures? Should you 'examine' what I wrote in this chapter?

I wrote a facebook status about the kataluma, inn keeper, and inn thoughts. One lady responded, "Not something I want in a Bible study. I am much more interested in how I can apply the teachings of God to my life today. Inn? No inn? I don't care." A.) I actually still kept her as a facebook friend. B.) I'm glad I believe in myself enough to not let her words majorly affect me. C.) Do you feel the same way? Do you even *care* about whether or not we all have the correct interpretation of the Christmas story?

Does it matter where Jesus was born? Hotel/motel/family home? Could you imagine Jesus looking down at us all doing our Christmas pageants and thinking, "That is sooo not the way I came into the world!"

Have you ever done a Bible study in which you had to examine the original language, customs, and traditions of the times in which the scripture was written? Did it change your views on any Bible passages?

There are some parables that Jesus taught, in which I

have heard that 'to the people, in that time', they completely understood what he was talking about, in contrast to our world and society now. Are there any Bible passages/teachings of Jesus that you can reference that are this same way?

Do you feel that it is wrong to question what the Bible says. If it says *inn*, it must mean a hotel/motel in Jesus' day, right? What if we have misunderstood passages in the Bible, because of wrong translation? Would that bother you to know we may have learned things wrong? Does it matter to you?

2 Timothy 2:15 tells us, "Study and be eager and do your utmost to present yourself to God approved (tested by trial), a workman who has no cause to be ashamed, correctly analyzing and accurately dividing [rightly handling and skillfully teaching] the Word of Truth." How much freedom do we have to dissect the Word of God? Are we not 'presentable' to God, if we have *not* 'analyzed' God's word? Is that something that should be left to pastors? How would you handle the situation if you knew a pastor had misinterpreted a portion of scripture? Would you confront that pastor? How would you do it? Do you have the biblical authority *to* question a pastor?

Have you ever read about or studied the feasts of the Old Covenant? Have you studied how Jesus fulfilled the feasts? Or will he fulfill them when he returns again? When do you think Jesus was conceived? Have you studied that before? Do you feel more comfortable with just sticking to the traditional date of December 25th? Why or why not?

Does the fact that the Catholic church decided to celebrate the birth of Christ on a pagan holiday, in order to get people into the church bother you? Or do you think it was rather genius of them? Is it wrong to celebrate his birth on a day *other than* the actual literal day? It was a *pagan* holiday. The opposite of Jesus. OK? Not OK? Thoughts?

Would you be more comfortable celebrating the birth of Jesus at a time separate from the long-standing date of December 25th, or would it just feel 'wrong'?

Ending Thought

A different version of the 2 Timothy 2:15 passage states, "Be diligent to present yourself approved to God, a worker who doesn't need to be ashamed, correctly teaching the word of truth." That last part: correctly teaching the word of truth is what speaks to me. To *me*, I interpret it as 'study, go deep, and know that what you are teaching is truth'.

I guess deep down, I am a truth seeker, and I desire for you to be one too. Does it matter where Jesus was born? I suppose not. The miracle is still there, whether in a motel room, and stinky barn, or the family home of Joseph. The *fact* that he came to this earth is what is important. And I get that. What bothers me is when people just assume something to be 'gospel truth' without researching it themselves.

One of my favorite Bible classes in college had our professor (on the very first day), stand up in front of this lecture hall and say, "Today, I want you to completely forget everything that you were taught in your Sunday school classes. Wipe it clean. Your salvation does not come from the fact that your parents are Christians and go to church on Sunday mornings. Your faith will now be built on what *you* believe because you will study this book (the Bible), do your research, testing, and you will now have your faith built on your own truths. You will *know that you know* because you have 'studied to show thyself approved'." Honestly, it was a life changing class.

Disagree with anything I have written in this Bible study? *Great*! Go research, dig into your Bible, find not only a certain verse, but the whole *context* of what a passage is saying. What scriptures come before it? After it? Is it a passage specifically meant for the people of that time, or does it transcend and relate and apply to us now over two thousand years later? What does the original language say? When you start digging *that* deep, it makes me a happy girl!

And I *do* love Christmas! Every part of it! Perhaps the next time you set out your nativity scene, complete with the Wise Men (who were almost certainly not present at the birth of Jesus), you will think of me and this CHAT.

tree toppers

"You have to see them with Sprit eyes." I have heard that line from people who claim that they have actually seen a 'live' angel. And I literally heard someone say to me, "They're in the back of the sanctuary. Can't you *see* them?" *I COULDN'T SEE THEM!* And I'm telling you, I *really* wanted to see the angels standing in the back!

It's almost as if it's an Elitist Club. The Angel See-ers. *'For only those who can use their Sprit Eyes.'* The cool kids. Who doesn't want to be in the cool club? And just what exactly *are* 'spirit eyes'? Makes me think of Mr. Potato Head, and the different sets of 'eyes' he stored in his 'nether region' compartment.

Have *you* ever seen an angel? I'm always kind of fascinated by the supernatural realm. I know that it's simply another dimension that we can't see with our limited human minds and eyes. We were created 'a little lower' than the angels (Psalm 8:5). There are things happening all around us that we physically can't see. But sometimes. *Some times* that curtain is temporarily lifted, and we humans can catch a glimpse into the world just beyond our senses. God gives us a few moments to see beyond our everyday, to experience where he daily dwells. The shepherds in Bethlehem experienced that awe and wonder on the night Jesus was born.

Honestly, could you *imagine* what the shepherds that night experienced? There previously had been angel sightings in the scriptures—but usually with just *one* angel. In the book of Luke, chapter one, starting with verse twenty-six, we are told that "In the sixth month, God sent the angel Gabriel to Nazareth, a town in Galilee, to a virgin pledged be married to a man named Joseph, a descendant of David. The virgin's name was Mary. The angel went to her and said, "Greetings, you who are highly favored! The Lord is with you."

Imagine being Mary, and seeing an angel for the first time, then receiving this (almost) unbelievable news. Yet that was just *one* angel. The shepherds saw a host. And that's a lot of angels.

"And there were shepherds living out in the fields nearby, keeping watch over their flocks at night. An angel of the Lord appeared to them, and the glory of the Lord shone around them, and they were terrified. But the angel said to them, 'Do not be afraid. I bring you good news that will cause great joy for all the people. Today in the town of David a Savior has been born to you; he is the Messiah, the Lord. This will be a sign to you: You will find a baby wrapped in cloths and lying in a manger.'

Suddenly a great company of the heavenly host appeared with the angel, praising God and saying, 'Glory to God in the highest heaven, and on earth peace to those on whom his favor rests.'"

Not just one angel. A host! So just how many angels *are* in a *host*? The Greek word for host (stratia) refers to "the heavenly bodies, stars of heaven--so called on account of their number and order." The heavenly host present at Jesus' birth were so numerous they were compared to the stars. Who can count the stars, much less number and order them, other than God?

The King James Version translates Luke 2:13 to say "a multitude of the heavenly host." Let's do the math. If one heavenly host is as numerous as the stars, how many is a *multitude* of heavenly host? Can't count that high.

In Genesis, when God was telling Abraham about all the decedents he will have, God told Abraham, "Look up at the sky and count the stars--if indeed you can count them." Only God can count how many stars and galaxies there are—just as only God could have counted the hosts of angels that were praising God at that very moment in time.

But we can imagine, right? I have been in arenas where there were thousands of people. I know what 'thousands' looks and sounds like. I have never been in a setting with tens of thousands, or hundreds of thousands yet alone a 'host'. But with my finite mind, I can't even imagine what it could have been like that night in Bethlehem.

So this was something new? More than one angel appearing to humans? Angels are mentioned at least 108 times in the Old Testament, and 165 times in the New Testament. For all of you math majors out there, I am going to solve that mathematical equation. That's *over* 273 times the Bible mentions angelic beings.

The Prophet Elijah's successor, Elisha was able to see angels. Not just one, but many. Not necessarily a 'multitude of hosts', but enough to fill the hillsides. There are just so many cool stories in the Bible, and this is one of them.

So the King of Aram was harassing the Israelites. The King knew of Elisha, and the fact that Elisha was telling the King of *Israel* things that the *King of Aram* spoke in private. (Side note: that would be a pretty cool spiritual gift.) So, at night the King of Aram sent men on horses and chariots to capture Elisha. They surrounded the city where Elisha was.

"When the servant of the man of God got up and went out early the next morning, an army with horses and chariots had surrounded the city. "Oh no, my lord! What shall we do?" the servant asked. "Don't be afraid," the prophet answered. "Those who are with us are more than those who are with them."

And Elisha prayed, "Open his eyes, Lord, so that he may see." Then the Lord opened the servant's eyes, and he looked and saw the hills full of horses and chariots of fire (ANGELS!) all around Elisha." (2 Kings 6:15-17)

I love that! So apparently, there *is* something to that whole 'spirit eyes' thing. Wouldn't *you* want to be able to see angels? I do.

I know that the Bible tells us that some of us have 'entertained angels' without knowing it (Hebrews 13:2). But not many have seen scores of angels all at once. It's interesting that God is particular to whom he allows to see multitudes of angels.

I'm sure there were other people in the city the day that Elisha prayed his servants' eyes would be opened. But why didn't *everyone* in the city get to see those angels at the same time? They were *there*, but for some reason only Elisha and his servant were privileged enough to actually, physically see them.

I think the same thing about the shepherds in Bethlehem the night Jesus was born. If the heavens opened up enough for *multitudes* of *hosts* to be seen, I'm thinking there was a *huge* opening in the sky at that moment. Surely the few shepherds out in the field weren't the only ones out and about that night? And if the sky was humongous enough for *all those angels* to be seen by the shepherds, I would think that heavenly portal/opening would have been big enough for people in neighboring towns and even into Jerusalem to see. Why didn't they?

I have absolutely no idea. How's that for a Bible study writer's answer? It's completely fascinating. And there is no answer. God himself tells us that, "'For My thoughts are not your thoughts, Nor are your ways My ways,' declares the LORD. 'For as the heavens are higher than the earth, So are My ways higher than your ways And My thoughts than your thoughts.'" (Isaiah 55:8-9)

So there's our answer. God's ways and thoughts are different from ours. We don't know why he does some of the things he does. No idea why only the shepherds that night saw the multitudes of angels, and not the entire city. But it's what happened. And God opened their 'spiritual eyes'. (I *so* want some of them!)

We do know that angels are messengers. The word angel actually comes from the Greek word *aggelos*, which means "messenger." The matching Hebrew word *mal'ak* has the same meaning. Messengers of God. Yes, there are the angels that worship around the throne of God in Heaven, but the angels that enter this realm have many different positions.

Here's the list of what they do: give messages, guide, provide, protect, deliver, strengthen, encourage, answer prayer, care for believers at the moment of death, and execute people.

I know, that last one is a harsh one. The Angel of Death killed every firstborn son in Egypt, *and* every firstborn livestock. Not my favorite image of an angel. But it happened. And there's another mass annihilation mentioned in Second Kings. But this is a Christmas study, so I won't go into that bloody mess right now.

Between the Old Testament and the New Testament there are approximately four hundred of what are called the 'silent years'. No major (or minor prophets) spoke or wrote. No great Kings of Israel. At least we aren't told of any.

Four hundred years of only hearing stories of what God had done in the past. Tales passed down from generation to generation. Until an angel broke that silence and made an announcement to Zechariah. And not just *any* angel, Gabriel. One of the big guys. His name means 'the strength of God'. We are told that he is an Archangel. A chief angel. A leader of the angels. Gabriel was who God specifically chose to break his silence for all those years. The time had come. And the prophecies of the Old Testament were about to be fleshed out.

Gabriel had a message, but he also had power to shut the mouth of Zechariah for unbelief. As one of nearly 20,000 Jewish priests, Zechariah served at the temple in Jerusalem for two one-week periods each year. A priest could offer the incense at the daily sacrifice only once in his lifetime. It was literally his once in a lifetime opportunity! Smoke of the incense symbolized prayers going to heaven. People were praying. Zechariah was undoubtedly praying.

Then the Archangel appears, and the first words he says are, "Do not be afraid, Zechariah. Your prayer has been heard." I love that he doesn't say prayers, but rather the singular, prayer. Zechariah had that one chance to be directly before God, and he took that opportunity to ask for an heir. A son.

Little did he know that his singular prayer would set in motion, that which was planned before the beginning of time. That this baby boy that he so desperately prayed for would be the forerunner of

Jesus Christ. That his son, John, would publically announce to the world who Jesus was.

Gabriel continued to tell Zechariah, "Your wife Elizabeth will bear you a son, and you are to call him John. He will be a joy and delight to you, and many will rejoice because of his birth, for he will be great in the sight of the Lord. He is never to take wine or other fermented drink, and he will be filled with the Holy Spirit even before he is born. He will bring back many of the people of Israel to the Lord their God. And he will go on before the Lord, in the spirit and power of Elijah, to turn the hearts of the parents to their children and the disobedient to the wisdom of the righteous—to make ready a people prepared for the Lord."

There's so much great stuff in that announcement. First off, this was (obviously) *way* before sonograms. To know the gender of your yet-to-be-fertilized child? Unbelievable! And a *son*, no less. One to carry on the family name and heritage. But the most fascinating detail of this announcement is that Gabriel stated that (even while he was still in the womb) John would be filled with the Holy Spirit.

This had never happened before. According to what I studied (and please, feel free to study this point more if you wish), no one had personally experienced the *indwelling* of the Holy Spirit prior to Pentecost. (OK, technically, the Virgin Mary did...but not an ongoing 'indwelling'). Leading of the Holy Spirit? Yes. But the indwelling into man happened after Jesus ascended into Heaven. Except for John the Baptist.

What an incredible announcement Gabriel was privileged to make. I'm sure all of Heaven was rejoicing as they got to see the unveiling of God's plan for redemption. I know that the Bible teaches us that "With the Lord a day is like a thousand years, and a thousand years are like a day" (II Peter 3:8), but still. The angels had waited *forever* to be able to make all of these exciting announcements. What anticipation! The time had come. And to those shepherds that were on duty with the sheep that night, wow. Talk about being in the right place at the right time!

We aren't told the name of the angel that announced the birth of Jesus to the shepherds. But I am sure when the heavens opened up, they were *all there*!

And these angels don't look like the little cherub figurines we have sitting around our houses on little shelves. Angels aren't baby-looking and dimple cheeked. They're strong warriors. These angels have 'eyes of fire'.

In the book of Daniel, Daniel himself describes an angel, "I looked up and there before me was a man dressed in linen, with a belt of fine gold from Uphaz around his waist. His body was like topaz, his face like lightning, his eyes like flaming torches, his arms and legs like the gleam of burnished bronze, and his voice like the sound of a multitude."

And I'm going to take a wild guess, and propose that actual angels do not have the appearance of the frilly, feminine, sweet, tender angels that typically adorn the top of Christmas trees. No wonder one of the first thing angels say is, "Fear not". That's a strong, tough being. The whole sky was filled with those beings proclaiming, "Glory to God in the highest, And on earth peace among men with whom He is pleased."

And that was just the *beginning* of the first day of Jesus' life. What a baby announcement!

Chat Time

Have you ever seen an actual angel? When? Where? Circumstances? What did it look like?

Have you experienced something where you wondered later if a 'person' you were in contact with had actually been an angel? What were the actions of that person/angel? Did that being say anything to you?

What do you think about 'seeing with spirit eyes'? Do you know anyone who sees angels on a regular basis? What is the difference between spirit eyes, and 'normal' eyes?

What do you imagine an angel looks like? Can people that die become an angel? Where do you think the term 'he just got his angel wings' when someone dies, came from?

Why do you think God chooses to reveal angelic beings to certain people, and not others? Do you think we see angels on a regular basis, but just don't realize it?

Have you ever read Frank Peretti's books, Piercing The Darkness or This Present Darkness? They were two of the first Christian fiction books (published in the

1980's) that dealt with angels and demons. I, personally, didn't think much of the whole angelic/demonic realm before reading those novels. What did you think of those books? Do you ever catch yourself thinking about those realms?

So how do we handle this 'Angel of Death'? Why do you think God has an angel that killed people and livestock? Doesn't the purpose of this angel seem against the characteristics of God? Do you ever think of this 'angel' when you imagine cherub little baby-type angels?

I posted the question, "Have you ever seen an angel" on my facebook page. *Many* people replied, "Yes!" A few people said they believed they saw an angel that had the resemblance of a deceased loved one. Have you ever experienced that? Do you think angels can take on the appearance of someone that has died? Why would they do that? Is it biblical? Can an angel appear as a woman, or are they strictly male in appearance?

When Gabriel made his announcement to Zechariah, Zechariah said, "How can I be sure of this? I am an old man and my wife is well along in years." Immediately Gabriel said, "I am Gabriel. I stand in the presence of God (*there's something about that 'I stand in the presence of God' line that I just LOVE. It's so very James Bond-ish/tough guy*), and I have been sent to speak to you and to tell you this good news. And now you will be silent and not able to speak until the day this happens, because you did not believe my words, which will come true at their appointed time."

Why do you think Zechariah got that harsh sentencing from Gabriel? What had he done wrong? Was it because God doesn't like doubters? What do you think would have happened if Zechariah was able to still talk? Do you think he could have talked himself out of the blessing of a son if had been able to verbally talk still?

Proverbs 18:21 tells us that our tongues hold the power of life and death. Perhaps, if Zechariah continued to verbally doubt what Gabriel said, that the plan set forth with John being Jesus' predecessor wouldn't have come about? What do you think? Can 'man', by speaking negatively, alter our own futures?

Have you ever talked yourself out of a blessing? Have you ever verbally doubted what God was doing with your life? If God had been able to make *you* mute, do you think your lack of verbalizing your doubt and negativity could have 'saved' you going down a path of non-blessing?

Are you a glass half full, or glass half empty kind of person? Obviously the power of our words and doubt vs. belief is powerful. Powerful enough that the angel Gabriel could not let Zechariah speak any doubt to Elizabeth, or those around him. Has there been a time in your life that you doubted you were good enough for God to bless you? Why? What were the circumstances?

If an angel came to you today, and gave you a message, do you think you would readily accept it? Would you also doubt? Or have you learned from all of the biblical examples we have been given? Would you think that you were completely 'losing it'? And doubt the reality of what you heard and saw?

Why do you think the host of angels announced the birth of Jesus to only those few shepherds? Don't you think an announcement of that magnitude should have been broadcast to people everywhere? At least to all of Bethlehem? What would have happened if the whole town of Bethlehem heard that announcement?

Ending Thought

I can't believe that chat christmas is over already. It went way too fast. I hope that as you read and discussed the topics in this book, God's word came a bit (or a *lot*!) more alive to you.

I have always been fascinated with angels. Created God-beings that are always there, but you just can't see them. Unbelievable. Yet, as Christians who believe God's word to be truth, we *must* believe that they are real. Some people see them. Some people don't. While other people have experiences that they can't explain other than, 'an angel came to my recue'.

People who have seen angels are afraid at first, yet angels bring messages from God *himself* who is full of peace. There are fallen angels and angels still with God. I still can't fathom why an angel would follow one of its own, and leave Heaven and the presence of their creator. See? Fascinating. They abide in a world just beyond our human senses. Yet one day we will live every day of our 'forever' surrounded by these beings.

And to think of their excitement of that first Christmas morning, when they got to break through that veil barrier to announce to the humblest of men in the grandest way possible that their *Savior*, the one who would redeem mankind, was within their reach. What joy. What beauty. What a message. Merry

Christmas everyone.

May this Christmas season be the most amazing ever. May God's presence be just a breath away. And in the midst of busyness and traditions, and family, may you find yourself wrapped up in the tangible love God has for you. That's why we take a tiny slice of every year to focus on the miracle of Jesus' birth. It started it all. In the most humble of ways, the most beautiful life began.

chat snacks

So this is just a fun little extra section. Here are some of my favorite dessert recipes. CHAT is based around conversation with one another, and what better to have with a good conversation, but yummy snacks! Of course, you don't have to make these goodies. But, from experience, these recipes tend to bring out the 'chat' in people I have served them to. Enjoy!

homemade cobbler
(apple, berry, or peach--)

*If making apple, follow this:
-One can apple pie filling
-Peel and thinly slice 4-5 fresh apples
-Combine the apple pie filling with the fresh apples. Add in some cinnamon, nutmeg, apple pie seasoning,

and about a ½ cup of brown sugar
-Place in a 'sprayed' 9x13 pan
-Buy two slice and bake sugar cookie rolls. Slice them, and layer them one row at a time on top of the apple mixture.
-Sprinkle cinnamon and white sugar on top
-Bake @ 350 for approx. 20 minutes. Watch so that the cookies don't burn
-Serve with vanilla ice cream
**For peach cobbler follow the same steps, except substitute peach pie filling and fresh peaches.
**For berry cobbler follow same steps, except use blackberry or raspberry pie filling with fresh blueberries, blackberries, and/or raspberries.
**So easy and SO good!

chocolate chip cookie layered dessert

This is so easy, but tastes so good!

Ingredients:
Two packages store-bought chocolate-chip cookies
Large tub of Cool Whip
Jar of fudge ice cream topping
French vanilla coffee creamer (liquid)

Directions:
-Use a 9x13 pan

-Pour the creamer into a bowl
-Dip each cookie in the creamer, and make a bottom layer of cookies in the pan
-Heat the fudge, and drizzle over the cookie layer
-Spoon a layer of Cool Whip over the fudge
-Repeat with dipped cookies and Cool Whip until the pan is full (or you run out of cookies)
-For fun, sprinkle chocolate chips, shaved chocolate, or sprinkles on top
-Cover and freeze
-Let it set for a few hours, then it's ready to cut and serve!

homemade box cake

This is a great cake recipe. And it starts simply, from a boxed cake mix. I use either vanilla, or chocolate, or devil's food cake mix—depending on what I'm in the mood for!

Ingredients:
One box cake mix
4 eggs
1 (3.9 oz.) Pudding mix (either vanilla or chocolate)
½ cup vegetable oil
½ cup water
1 cup sour cream
Semi-sweet chocolate chips

Directions:

-Mix all the ingredients together (fold in chocolate chips)

-Spray a Bundt pan and pour in batter

-Bake @ 350 for an hour. Watch to not burn the top. (Put foil over the top if it's starting to brown too much)

*This cake is so moist, it doesn't need frosting, but it's great with ice cream!

chocolate chip cheesecake ball

This is one of my absolute favorites EVER. And it makes enough to feed a lot of people. I have doubled the recipe before, to make two cheeseballs, or to just have at home for snacking!

Ingredients:

1 package 8oz. cream cheese

½ cup butter softened

½ tablespoon vanilla extract

¾ cup confectioners' sugar

2 tablespoons brown sugar

½ bag mini chocolate chips

*1/2 bag of mini chocolate chips

Chopped pecans

Directions:

-In a large bowl, beat the cream cheese, butter and vanilla until fluffy

-Gradually add sugars; beat just until combined. Stir in chocolate chips

-Cover and refrigerate for 2 hours

-Place cream cheese mixture on a large piece of plastic wrap; shape into a ball

-Refrigerate for at least 1 hour. Just before serving, roll cheese ball in pecans and mini chocolate chips.

*Serve with graham crackers, or Nilla wafers!

french coconut pecan bars

These are just way easy, and so good! I usually double the recipe, and bake them in a 'roaster pan'. I love buying the big aluminum bakers, so I don't have to bring a pan home to clean it. I just throw away the aluminum pan!

Ingredients:

¾ cup butter or margarine, melted

1 (18.25-oz.) pkg. French Vanilla Cake Mix

1 egg

2 ½ cups quick-cooking rolled oats

1 (15-oz.) can Coconut Pecan Frosting

1 (12-oz.) pkg. (2 cups) semisweet chocolate chips

½ cup chopped pecans

Directions:

-Heat oven to 350°F. Spray 15x10x1-inch baking pan with nonstick cooking spray.

-Place melted butter in large bowl. Reserve 3 tablespoons of the cake mix; set aside. Add remaining cake mix to butter; blend well.

-Add egg; mix well. Stir in oats. Press 2/3 of cake mix mixture (about 2 1/2 cups) in bottom of sprayed pan

- Place frosting in medium microwave-safe bowl; microwave on HIGH for 1 minute. Add reserved 3 tablespoons cake mix; stir until large lumps disappear

- Drizzle half of frosting mixture over cake mix mixture in pan; spread evenly

-Sprinkle with chocolate chips and pecans. Drizzle with remaining frosting mixture

-Crumble remaining cake mix mixture over frosting mixture

- Bake at 350°F. for 25 to 30 minutes or until top is golden brown and edges are bubbly. Cool 1 1/2 hours or until completely cooled. Cut into bars.

mile-high peanut butter brownie pie

You must pinkie promise me that you will only use Ghirardelli brownie mix for this pie. Because believe-you-me, it's the best that way! And you might as well double the recipe. It's that good.

chat christmas

Ingredients:
1 Pillsbury® refrigerated pie crust, softened as directed on box
1 package Ghirardelli Brownie Mix
1/3 cup vegetable oil
3 tablespoons water
1 egg
1 (8 ounce) package cream cheese, softened
1/2 cup creamy peanut butter
1 cup powdered sugar
1 (8 ounce) container frozen whipped topping, thawed
2 tablespoons mini semi-sweet chocolate chips

Directions:
-Heat oven to 350 degrees F. Unroll pie crust; place in ungreased 9-inch glass pie plate as directed on box for One-Crust Filled Pie; flute edge.
-In medium bowl, stir brownie mix, oil, water and with spoon. Pour batter into crust-lined pie plate.
-Bake 30 to 40 minutes, covering edge of crust with strips of foil after 15 to 20 minutes, until crust is golden brown and center of brownie is set. Cool slightly, about 20 minutes. Refrigerate 1 hour or until completely cooled.
-In medium bowl, beat cream cheese, peanut butter and powdered sugar with electric mixer on medium speed until smooth.
-Fold in whipped topping. Spread mixture over brownie. Sprinkle chocolate chips. Refrigerate before serving. Store covered in refrigerator.

chocolate chip ooey gooey buttercake

Ingredients:
(Crust)
1 box butter recipe cake mix
1 egg
(1/2 c butter, melted
Filling)
1 8oz. pkg cream cheese, softened
2 eggs
1 tsp. pure vanilla extract
1 16oz box powdered sugar
1/2c butter, melted
1 c. chocolate chips

Directions:
-Preheat oven to 350 degrees. Lightly grease a 9x13 inch baking pan.
-In a bowl, combine cake mix, egg, and butter with an electric mixer. Mix well.
-Pat into the bottom of prepared pan and set aside.
-Still using an electric mixer, beat cream cheese until smooth, add eggs and vanilla. Dump powdered sugar and beat very well.
-Reduce the speed of mixer and slowly pour in melted butter
-Stir in the chocolate chips.
-Pour filling onto cake mixture and spread evenly.
-Bake for 40-50 minutes
-Remove from oven and allow to cool completely. If

you want to drizzle melted chocolate over the top allow it to cool for at least 15 minutes then you can drizzle. Let set for at least another hour and then cut into bars.

coconut cake

Can you tell that I am a lover of easy and good dessert recipes? This is another one! This was my Father-in-Law's favorite cake.

Ingredients:
One box white cake mix
*Eggs, oil, water (as specified on the box)
One can of coconut cream
Bag of shredded coconut
Large tub of Cool Whip

Directions:
-Make cake according to directions. Add in half the bag of coconut
-Bake in 9x13 pan
-When cake comes out of oven, poke all over with a fork
-Pour the coconut cream over the top of the cake, making sure it gets soaked into the holes
-Refrigerate cake
-Mix the remaining shredded coconut with the tub of Cool Whip and 'frost' on top
-Keep refrigerated, then serve

*This is one of those cakes that is actually better the next day, after the coconut cream has set in. So good!

butterfinger cake

This is the same type of cake as the coconut. Starts with a boxed cake mix. My son's request this cake!

Ingredients:
Box of French vanilla cake
*Egg, oil, water (as specified on the box)
Jar of butterscotch ice cream topping
1 can sweetened condensed milk
Large tub of Cool Whip
4 large Butterfinger candy bars

Directions:
-Follow the directions on the cake box. Bake in a 9x13 pan
-When the cake comes out of the oven, poke thoroughly with a fork
-Pour the sweetened condensed milk, then the butterscotch topping over the cake, making sure it gets soaked into the holes
-Refrigerate cake
-'Frost' the cake with Cool Whip
-Sprinkle crushed Butterfingers over the top
-Keep refrigerated

'easy' layered ice cream cake

This is another EASY recipe that looks so fancy and tastes great.

Ingredients:
Box of ice cream sandwiches, unwrapped
Large tub of Cool Whip (2?)
Jar (or 2?) of hot fudge ice cream topping
*Optional, peanuts

Directions:
-In a 9x13 pan, make a bottom layer of ice cream sandwiches
-Microwave for a minute, then pour the hot fudge over the ice cream sandwiches
-*Sprinkle with peanuts
-Add a layer of Cool Whip
-Repeat ice cream bar layer
-Add a top layer of Cool Whip
-*Sprinkle peanuts over top
*Cut into squares to serve. SO easy, yet looks very impressive!

no bake cookies

They're not fancy. They're easy, simple, old fashioned, and just so good. (Double the recipe to bring to your CHAT group!)

Ingredients:
1 3/4 cups white sugar
1/2 cup milk
1/2 cup butter
4 tablespoons unsweetened cocoa powder
1/2 cup crunchy peanut butter
3 cups quick-cooking oats
1 teaspoon vanilla extract

Directions:
-In a medium saucepan, combine sugar, milk, butter, and cocoa. Bring to a boil, and cook for 1 1/2 minutes.
-Remove from heat, and stir in peanut butter, oats, and vanilla.
-Drop by teaspoonful onto wax paper. Let cool until hardened.

butterscotch haystack cookies

My boys love these cookies too! So easy. So good!

Ingredients:
1 2/3 cups (11-oz. pkg.) Butterscotch Flavored Morsels

3/4 cup creamy peanut butter
1 can (8.5 oz.) or 2 cans (5 oz. each) Chow Mein noodles
3 1/2 cups miniature marshmallows

Directions:
-MICROWAVE morsels in large, uncovered, microwave-safe bowl on MEDIUM-HIGH (70%) power for 1 minute; STIR. The morsels may retain some of their original shape. If necessary, microwave at additional 10- to 15-second intervals, stirring just until morsels are melted.
-Stir in peanut butter until well blended.
-Add Chow Mein noodles and marshmallows; toss until all ingredients are coated.
-Drop by rounded tablespoon onto prepared trays.
-Refrigerate until ready to serve.

my all-time favorite chocolate chip cookie recipe!

I can't take the credit for these cookies, but I will take the credit for passing on this recipe to you! I have made these for over 24 years. Best consistency and flavor out there! A full recipe works best, and leaves you will some to keep and plenty to share!

Ingredients:
Cream together:

Kirsten Hart

1 lb. butter
1 box dark brown sugar
1 ½ c. white sugar
Beat together, the add:
2 tablespoons pure vanilla extract
3 eggs
Beat together. Then combine and mix in:
5 ½ c. flour
1 ½ tsp. baking soda
1 ½ tsp. salt
Fold in:
2 (12 oz.) bags of semi-sweet chocolate chips
2 ½ c. nuts (optional)

Additional directions:
Line baking sheet with non-stick foil. Bake at 275
degrees for 18-20 minutes The lower temperature is
the key!

About The Author

Kirsten Hart has been able to travel with some of America's premier Christian singing groups, including Re-Creation, Eternity, The Spurrlows, FRIENDS (the back-up group for Grammy Award winner Larnelle Harris), The Richard Roberts TV Singers, as a Praise and Worship Leader for International Crusades, and on TBN's This Is Your Day telecast. Since moving to Branson, Missouri, she has been a part of DINO Kartsonakis' Christmas Spectacular Show, as well as his Tribute To The Titanic production.

She has had the amazing opportunity to sing on television, in hundreds of churches, and as part of international crusades. She has shared her heart before thousands. She also counts it a privilege to have sung and spoken for Focus On the Family, Compassion International events, Campmeetings, Statewide Conventions, and more.

Kirsten has spoken in churches and for Women's Ministry Events across the country for the past twenty years. Her previous books include Kirsten Hart's Beauty Secrets, Born For This, and Baby Girl Murphy. CHAT, and CHAT teens. To find out more about this author, visit her website, www.kirstenhart.com.

Made in the USA
Columbia, SC
01 November 2018